why wish you a
merry Christmas?

why wish you a merry Christmas?

What matters (and what doesn't)
in the festive season

NICK BAINES

CHURCH HOUSE
PUBLISHING

Church House Publishing
Church House
Great Smith Street
London SW1P 3AZ

ISBN 978-0-9562821-0-1

Published 2009 by Church House Publishing
in association with St Andrew Press

The opinions expressed in this book are those of the author and do not
necessarily reflect the official policy of the General Synod or The
Archbishops' Council of the Church of England.

Printed in England by CPI Bookmarque, Croydon CR0 4TD

CONTENTS

INTRODUCTION

Christmas seems to come round quickly these days. No sooner have the Easter eggs been digested than the Christmas juggernaut starts rolling. Yes, there are still the summer holidays to get out of the way before the nights start drawing in, but the shops and the telly are already starting to drop the odd bit of tinsel into the frame. And, whether you want one or not, there's seemingly no escape.

Get into the autumn and something in the back of your head starts to echo with the faint hint of a perennial mantra. It could be Noddy Holder screaming 'Merry Christmas' down a microphone he probably shouldn't have swallowed. Or the spectre of Johnny Mathis pondering the consequences 'when a child is born'. Or Cliff Richard combining mistletoe and wine and wondering why it tastes funny. Or (and I realize this could keep going for a very long time through a very long line of singers and songs) Mud promising optimistically that you'll be 'lonely this Christmas' – just the thing you want to hear when the leaves are dropping off the trees, the evenings are getting darker, the weather is getting wetter and your empty bank account promises to turn red with embarrassment.

Christmas is coming. And it is coming with what Baldrick might have called 'the inevitability of something inevitable'. It can't be avoided, so we watch its approach either with pleasure or dread.

Well, I'm an easy man to find on Christmas morning. I am usually in prison. It is the custom in the Diocese of Southwark for the bishops to spend Christmas morning in Brixton, Wandsworth or Belmarsh and we usually enjoy the experience. But I always face a particular challenge when greeting prisoners who come to the service and sing carols and think about what they might be missing back at home: family, children, food and drink and so on. I look them in the eye and wish them 'happy Christmas' and then wonder what on earth that is supposed to mean to someone in their circumstances. It might just be my problem and entirely natural to those who reciprocate in kind. But, 'happy Christmas' sounds pretty trite and inappropriate to me when meeting people locked up in prison and separated from the people they most want to be with.

What, in God's name, can be 'happy' about Christmas if the circumstances are lousy and everything about it reinforces the fact that you are excluded from the public or family celebration? And 'celebration' of what? Of some vague sentimental feeling about babies and angels? Or of special stars in the sky and the exchanging of gifts that cost you an arm and a leg, but might not be wanted in the first place?

I think people approach Christmas with very different feelings depending on what the rest of life holds for them. If you are short of cash or the job has disappeared, it could fill you with dread – especially if you've got dependants to provide for. If you are lonely anyway, the threat of spending the 'happy days' alone while everyone else is apparently celebrating and living it up is hardly an attractive one. Yet, on the other hand, if life is proving to be a bit rubbish, the promise of a bit of artificial snow-coated escapism might offer a glimpse of brightness to an otherwise gloomy prospect.

The recent economic downturn has seen hundreds of thousands of people lose their jobs, families staring into the abyss of unemployment and loss of income, status and prospects. People who thought their life was set on an ever-upward trajectory have seen it all collapse in front of their eyes. For many people this Christmas will simply ram home the fact that they can't afford what they used to be able to buy – that life has changed materially. And the pressure this puts on relationships, families and the values we thought we cherished is incalculable.

And it is not just the loss of 'real' things that makes a difference. Even for those whose lives have remained reasonably unaffected by the fallout of the global financial disaster, the world has changed for ever. It has now become clear that the whole world existed on the basis of trust and confidence. We trusted the banking system and we had confidence in those who ran it. Now we discover that the trust was misplaced and, consequently, the confidence has evaporated. So, doesn't Christmas just rub salt in the wounds?

This book is intended to say the opposite. All sorts of fantasies have grow up around Christmas and it has been sentimentalized into the sort of anaemic tameness that has made many people think of it as nothing more than some sort of a fairy story – which is nothing short of tragic, because nothing could be further from the truth. The Christmas story, which has become all too familiar to many of us, contains the roots of hope for individuals as well as societies. A bold claim? Well, maybe. But let's have a go and see if the story we read in the Gospels has anything to say to us in a western country at the beginning of the twenty-first century. Christmas is actually about God taking the real world seriously and getting stuck into it – getting his hands dirty in the real business of complicated lives and often mucky systems. If we find ourselves in a place of confusion, bewilderment or anger about the way the world has gone, we might even find ourselves surprised by what the Christmas story has to say about God, the world and us.

In this short book, I plan to take you on a thought-provoking and, I hope, entertaining personal journey through all the usual ups and downs, cultural norms of the typical Christmas experience and look at things: Christmas pop songs, carols, snow, family get-together, nativity plays, presents. In the process, there'll be questions that offer a fresh perspective on routines that may have become tired ones.

My hope is really quite simple: that in reading this book, you might be able to hear the Christmas story through refreshed ears, consider its meaning anew and find encouragement that a Christian understanding of God's commitment to his world and its people is powerful – and includes you. All you need to bring to it is curiosity. After all, this is a story about God being down to earth. The least we can do is join him down here and engage our imagination.

DREAMING OF A WHITE CHRISTMAS

February 2009 in England was fantastic. I have lived in and visited different parts of the world and experienced all sorts of extreme weather. But living in London doesn't exactly expose us to the meteorological dramas that some places get. If it snows in London, it is just a sort of weak flurry that melts as soon as it hits the ground. It gets cold . . . ish, but it's not exactly the biting, bone-freezing cold of the Russian steppe. The wind might blow a bit and the gritter lorries might trundle out for the odd night of half-hearted dribbling down the main roads, but it never lasts very long.

In February 2009 all that changed. For two glorious days it snowed and snowed and snowed. In my garden in Croydon we measured twelve inches of the white stuff and it shocked the entire transport system into a complete shut-down. People couldn't get to work and plans for re-building the recession-hit economy were subjected to the more pleasurable and guilt-free priority of building snowmen, sledging down any available slope and lobbing snowballs at anyone who was stupid enough to stand still for long enough to become a target. It was just great fun.

The landscape was transformed into a quiet and beautiful dreamland. Even built-up Croydon looked like a Christmas card scene and everyone who ventured outside couldn't help themselves letting slip a smile to complete strangers, however hard they tried to suppress such public expressions of emotion.

But, what was the use of all this snow in February? Where was it when we needed it – at Christmas? After all, we send each other

Christmas cards with Victorian snow scenes and sweet little robins, and people even place bets on it being a white Christmas. Go into any department store and you can't escape the droning and comforting loveliness of Bing Crosby 'dreaming of a white Christmas'. Well, Bing Crosby obviously didn't live in England! It *never* snows at Christmas. Yet we still conjure up images of a romantic snow scene and try to live as if we were characters in some Victorian fantasy. I have even seen Australian Christmas cards with Victorian English snow scenes, sent by people having a yuletide barbecue on the beach on 25 December. What's that about?

Up to our knees in it

Why do we do this? I think one answer might actually be found in what happened in February 2009 when it snowed six weeks too late for the big event. Everything stopped, we gave up being driven by economics and we went out to play. In other words, we took the time to do something that has no purpose other than enjoyment in the company of other people who have also had no alternative but to relax and take a breather from the world. We surrendered to the freedom of pointless frolicking in the park and put behind us for a moment the relentless drivenness of daily work and pressure. Perhaps we were experiencing what our ancestors discovered when they enshrined one day a week as an inviolable pause in the progress of what the English poet Andrew Marvell called 'time's winged chariot' – space for rest and play and reorienting ourselves for the future. It is a way of stopping, looking around, checking where we are going (and why we are going there in the first place) and making sure we are headed in the right direction.

A second reason why we romanticize Christmas and collude in the white myth is what the Scottish theologian and musician, John

Bell, has called 'teddy bear theology'. I'd better explain.

If you ask me what I remember about growing up in Liverpool in the early 1960s – and especially about Christmas during those years – I will flood you with memories. They will include memories of struggling up Sunnybank Road with the snow drifts up to my waist, the road impassable and the neighbours building snowmen in their gardens. I will regale you with reminiscences of the whole of Liverpool grinding to a halt, of happy children and me coming home to a warm coal fire and the comforting familiarity of a cosy house. The trouble is, however, that I am not sure it ever happened. Yes, it once snowed enough in Sunnybank Road for the drifts to be over my knees – but I was probably only about three feet tall at the time. I have no idea what the reality was, but I am assured it didn't happen at Christmas, didn't last long . . . and that we probably had gas-fired central heating by then anyway.

We don't deliberately romanticize the past in order to lie about it. Nor do we intend to fabricate a world that never actually existed. But, I think we do produce a simplified past experience against which we measure the messiness and complexities of our adult lives now. It is as if there is something in us that wants to go back to cuddling the teddy bear, reassuring us that all is well with the world, that we are safe and we don't have to worry too much about the future – just what we want for our children. We long for security and the irresponsibility of what we wish our childhood had represented.

The problem with this tendency is that we can easily lose touch with the real world and suppress the real experiences of our childhood. We want our own children to be sweet and innocent and unworried about the great complexities of modern living in the postmodern world. We want to protect them from the difficult choices adults have to make and from the consequences of the choices that we adults have already made. So, we create a romantic past that never existed and try to re-create the feelings we then associate with it.

The taming of Christmas

And what does all this have to do with Christmas? Well, we have managed, by romanticizing the festival and commercializing our culture, to turn Christmas into something tame, fantastic and anaemic. It has gradually become a festival without a content, a celebration without a reason and a form of escapism without the possibility of escape from the consequences of how we celebrate it. Even the reason for the season has got lost beneath the rattle of tills and the tinsel on the window ledge.

Losing the plot

A couple of years ago I was asked to lead an assembly in a primary school in South London. I was asked to take my episcopal staff (a real-deal shepherd's crook from the Lake District) and talk about the Christmas story. Naturally, I thought I'd do the shepherds; but, I needed a way in – a way to get the children thinking along the right lines before I told the story. So, I asked the 300 or so children what I thought was a simple question: 'Who is the most important character in the Christmas story?' The hands shot up (as they always do in a primary school assembly). I pointed to a little girl and she looked scared before lowering her hand again – but at least she didn't cry. I pointed to a little lad and he confidently answered my question: 'Santa Claus', he said. 'Great answer', I replied, 'but not the one I was looking for.' The next child was equally confident: 'The elves', he suggested. It wasn't going well. I went for a third child – an older lad who asked rather weakly if I was thinking of Cinderella.

At that point I decided it wasn't a great idea to ask such an open-ended question of school children. The teachers were standing round the hall looking simultaneously both amused and embarrassed.

What has happened here is that the children are bombarded with stories and images around the Christmas period, but without being given the tools to discriminate between what is fairy story, what is pantomime and what is about the birth of Christ. Every story is given the same value and so every story is relegated to fictional fantasy – or, at best, to some vague moral parable aimed at encouraging our children to be nice to each other.

I think this happens because those of us who grew up after the 1960s – and who are now teaching our children – managed the great intellectual and cultural achievement of chucking God out with Father Christmas. One fantasy figure with a big white beard got found out and the other one went out with him. So, we kept the Jesus story going – albeit with increasing remoteness and a certain embarrassment – but saw it as just one more story alongside the panto and fairy stories.

And going to a traditional carol service doesn't always help. Some of the traditional carols perpetuate images of Christmas that have more to do with Victorian sentiment than the story we actually read in the Gospels. For example, despite what we sing in the lovely 'Away in a Manger', baby Jesus probably *did* cry.

Recovering the plot

There is a terrible irony about all this. Stick baby Jesus in a manger with a tame cow in attendance and rather characterless parents looking bewildered by the whole thing and it just looks unreal – weird. But read the Gospels afresh (the accounts of the Christmas story and what led up to it can be found in the first two chapters of the Gospels of Matthew and Luke) and the events they record are all too real.

Here you have a young girl in an obscure village in the northern hills of an obscure part of the Roman Empire two millennia ago. The country is under military occupation and civil society is a seething mess of collaboration and rebellion, all infused with religious fervour and agonized questioning about national/religious identity and purpose. This young girl finds herself pregnant while engaged and, to cut a long story short, finds that rather than divorcing her, the older man to whom she is betrothed is still prepared to become her husband. They travel from the northern hills to Bethlehem in the south in order to register for a national census – in other words, to line up for the poll tax which supported the foreign forces of occupation.

The baby is born in the animals' compartment of an ordinary family home, probably surrounded by the attention of the women of the extended family. While still coming to terms with the birth of her firstborn, in a culture with a high infant mortality rate, the family is visited by working men from the hills and (probably much later and when they are back in Nazareth) by foreign star-gazers who bring odd and ominous gifts to the child.

Word gets out to the paranoid local ruler (Herod) and he sets about trying to eliminate any chance of any challenge from any human stupid enough to be thought of as a 'king'. Little boys get unjustly slaughtered as a consequence. Romantic?

So, what does that tell us – apart from the fact that it all sounds very real and very familiar to anyone who reads a newspaper or watches the television today? The Christmas story is set in a brutal and unjust world of real time and real space. Military power enforces political and economic systems that cannot be bucked. Political rebellion is all around, while ordinary people just keep on trying to do some work, make a living, feed their families and keep on going. They have to deal with profit and loss, poll taxes, unjust laws and uncertain futures. Parents have no idea what will become of their children – if their children ever survive to adulthood. Innocent families suffer at the bloodied hands of powermongers who cause unjust suffering to people who just want to get on with their lives. Life is tough and rough and every day is a struggle for survival. And into this reality a baby is born who promises something different. All the evidence of the world mocks the prospect of illusions such as 'hope'; yet in this child something unique might just happen.

But you have to leave Christmas behind and follow your curiosity to see what it is all about. And, if you think this is just for 'religious' people who are already 'that way inclined', just remember that the shepherds were regarded as riff-raff by polite society and the stargazers or magi would have been viewed as mere foreign heathen. So, you are in good company, if you just fancy seeing where all this leads to. It won't lead to a snow-white, fairy-tale or Victorian Christmas, but it might just make us pause in the frenzy of preparation and check our direction of travel.

2 WHO CHANGED THE SCRIPT?

When my children were very young I used to read them stories while they cuddled their teddy and sucked a well-tasted thumb in bed. This was a precious time of day: the hard business of playing in the garden, going to playgroup, eating food they didn't like was all in the past. The laughing and the crying were done and now sleep awaited. And the bedtime story was the last thing to happen before the eyes closed and the breathing slowed and the body relaxed.

With a bit of luck I woke up before the children noticed.

Actually, that is not too far from the truth.

From time to time I used to make up stories – asking the kids to suggest three or four key ingredients (random stuff such as a giant, a jar of mustard, a piece of paper and Liverpool Football Club) that I would have to get into an original story that was clever, exciting, mysterious and funny. No challenge there, then. I invented characters called mugglewumps, long before J. K. Rowling discovered her Muggles, and created imaginative stories that kept the children rapt till they slept. And that's where the trouble began.

Once they were asleep, I would move on to the evening's business and forget the story I had so carefully woven from the threads of my over-active imagination. Then, the next evening, I'd be asked to re-tell the story I'd invented the night before. And I couldn't remember how I'd told it. So, I'd give it a go and try to put the narrative back together again, but would meet a wall of outraged protest: I'd missed something or got things the wrong way round. It was as if I had ended *Little Red Riding Hood* with the little girl being eaten by her granny – or Cinderella beating the life out of her two prettier sisters because they had stolen her slippers. Living with young children teaches you that you cannot change the stories – that you have to get them right in every detail of content and form.

Maybe it is simply that the children are practising for later in life. After all, from childhood on, we get an idea of how we would like our lives to develop and we hope that it will all be all right. Adults constantly ask children what they want to be when they grow up – as if a child could possibly know not only what, but also how. It is as if we try to write a script that will make life interesting but predictable, secure but exciting, surprising but in a nice sort of way. And we don't cope very well when someone changes the script.

This is why the media report not what is 'normal' (good news), but generally headline what is 'abnormal' or unusual (bad or shocking news). It is always when the script is deviated from that we sit up and take notice. Most people assume that life will take a particular course and hope that everything will work out OK: parents should not outlive their children, our bodies should not get cancer, accidents should be prevented, good actions should not bring bad consequences. But things never go according to plan and real life involves coping with that, trying to navigate in uncharted waters as life throws at us what we hadn't expected it to.

So, pensioners saved all their money and carefully invested it, only to find that when the banks collapsed, so did their assumptions about their level of income in retirement. Young people leaving university with a good law degree suddenly found that the promise of a job in the city failed to materialize. The construction apprentice who had put years into learning his trade suddenly found that developers couldn't finance the development of their sites, so builders had no work and jobs were buried in the foundations of buildings that will no longer get built. All the promises and assumptions about the natural course of life and work have, for many people, gone out of the proverbial window, leaving them unsure about the future and no longer confident about the predictability of life's ordinary routines. Nothing, it seems, can be taken for granted any longer.

And this is where doing something as strange and unfashionable as recalling Bible stories might actually help us.

An unwanted pregnancy

The experience of interruption is actually the norm for most of the world's population. It always has been. We know this, of course, but we somehow don't expect it to affect our own lives. But it is a fact of life that the God of the Bible seems to take utterly seriously.

Way back at the beginning of the Old Testament in the Book of Genesis we read about an old man called Abram who had settled down for his retirement with his elderly wife, Sarai. Then God asked him to pack up all his stuff, take his family with him and set off for a destination that was unclear, but would be revealed as they went on their journey. It was a ridiculous invitation and yet it worked. Later on in the Old Testament the people are having a religious revival and allowing their corrupt leaders to forge all sorts of dodgy political and military alliances – all aimed at protecting their own power. Unheeded warnings from the prophets see the people's lives rudely interrupted as military occupation and exile follow. Their world falls apart and their whole way of understanding who they are (God's people) and where they are going is thrown into turmoil.

Come into the Christmas story and we find, again, a rude interruption in the 'normal' life and expectations of ordinary people.

Mary is a young girl – probably in her early teens. She lives in the hill country of the north and has been chosen by an older man called Joseph to be his wife. As was the usual custom, they were betrothed to be married and everyone would have assumed that the wedding would take place in due course, followed by the arrival of children who would grow up and become the pension fund for the parents and grandparents. Joseph would continue his carpentry business and Mary would do what women did. But, then something happened.

The routine of life in the northern village family was shattered by the realization that young Mary was pregnant. Joseph knew the child wasn't his and tried to find a way of getting out of the relationship without humiliating Mary. She must have been scared out of her wits. The shame of her teenage out-of-marriage pregnancy would have seen her in trouble with her family, the subject of gossip in the village community and an object of shame in public. All her expectations and hopes for an ordinary life simply evaporated.

Let's face it, it wasn't much better for Joseph. Not only was his planned marriage out of the question, but also his reputation in the community would have suffered. And there would always have been the gossip and unresolved suspicion – something he would just have to learn to live with. Might his business suffer because of questions about his own reliability or integrity? In a small community, how would he look people in the eye when he knew everyone was talking? His world fell apart and he didn't know what to do for the best. After all, there was no script for this and he had no guide to follow.

A hard day's night

But Mary and Joseph (and their respective families) weren't the only characters in the Christmas story to find their lives thrown into disarray by uninvited and deeply disturbing intrusions.

Luke tells us about some shepherds who were out in the fields doing what shepherds did. It is probable that each night was similar to the night before: not a lot happened and the sheep did what sheep do at night on a Palestinian hill. You can imagine the shepherds minding their own business and whiling away the time in conversation about the routines of their ordinary lives. In other words, probably not a lot was happening and this particular night was very similar to other unspectacular nights in the hills.

We don't really find out a great deal about these guys other than the fact that they were scared witless by the appearance of an angel surrounded by even more angels – a heavenly host – all of whom spoke to them rather directly. Not surprisingly they did not just take this in their stride, but went down into the town, leaving their sheep to fend for themselves, and sought out the baby that had just been born to Mary. They then went out and spread the word about what had happened, thus causing a degree of amazement and probably a lot of suspicion.

So, Mary and Joseph and the shepherds have at least this one thing in common: their ordinary lives are broken into and seriously messed up by uninvited disruptive elements. All their assumptions about the 'normal' world were thrown into disarray and they were now going to have to rethink how they thought about their lives and the way the world is.

But it still doesn't end with Mary, Joseph and the shepherds (of whom more later). In Matthew's account of the birth and early years of Jesus, some astrologers find themselves setting out on a journey from their homeland in the east (possibly what we now know as Iraq). They clearly aren't too sure where they are going, but they end up at a strange destination and in the midst of some dangerous political intrigue. Having innocently enquired of paranoid King Herod about the chances of finding in the neighbourhood a baby who is destined to be king, they have to think quickly and take evasive action to avoid being tricked into personal danger and the betrayal of a young and vulnerable family.

Unwelcome intrusions and weird gifts

The Christmas story, then, is not a sentimental one designed to provide future generations with an archetypical nativity tableau to keep parents and grandparents happy watching the sweet little children perform in church. It involves people whose lives are rudely and decisively interrupted. Just like us when the banks collapse, the job disappears, the savings lose their value, illness hits or bereavement shatters our life and expectations. All of us get used to thinking ahead and planning our lives as if everything will just carry on and keep going. Sudden interruptions are never welcome and almost always cause us grief.

But there is also a sense in which they can bring opportunities that could not come in any other way. After all, few if any of us would volunteer to have our lives broken into and our expectations thwarted. But this is how life always has been and always will be. We are not in ultimate control and have to decide how we will confront the unexpected interruptions that change our lives and challenge our thinking. Do we simply resent what has happened and go into 'victim' mode – or do we look for the ways in which we can accept the reality with which we are faced and then try to shape it? It is surely more healthy to shape one's own future than to go through life feeling like a victim of other people's choices or of the circumstances that occur. Isn't it?

As we have seen, shepherds had to leave their work and come to terms with weird encounters. The magi had to leave their home in order to be in a position to be surprised by the baby to whom they gave ominous gifts – the gold, frankincense and myrrh are signs of the suffering and death to come. The disciples of the adult Jesus would need to allow their routines and expectations to be cut across and then choose to follow Jesus along a beach and beyond. They had no idea where it would all lead, but the key bit was being brave or curious enough to start out and venture into the unknown.

This is key to the Christmas story and common to everybody's life experience. We want to be the author of our own script, but it never quite works out like that. We easily resent it when someone else edits it or slips in factors which make us change direction. But we can choose to go with the changed circumstances, add our own shaping to the mix – and even say 'yes' to the new opportunities thrown up by the new challenges, just as Mary found she was to be pregnant and said 'yes' to God.

But maybe we ought also to teach our children that real stories are never fixed and that endings can sometimes change unexpectedly and uncomfortably. At the very least, we shouldn't tell them about Christmas if we don't follow the story through to Easter.

3   MONEY MAKES THE WORLD GO AROUND (APPARENTLY)

I can't quite remember whether Abba did any songs about Christmas. If they did, I missed them. But, if I had to choose an Abba song to fit the Christmas spirit, it would have to be 'Money, money, money'. According to Agnetha, Benny, Björn, and Anni-Frid, 'it's a rich man's world' and finding a rich man would allow you to stop work and start fooling around for the rest of your life. Sounds brilliant, doesn't it? But what would you do all day once the novelty of 'stuff' had worn off and you realized the world was just the same as before? Well, I guess a good tune helps and that's what Abba provided.

If Abba can't really help us, perhaps we need to leave the pop charts and head for the musical theatre. And what do we find there? The final days of the Weimar Republic as the Nazis took over Germany in the 1920s and 30s are powerfully portrayed in the film and theatre productions of *Cabaret*. As the world becomes more violent and life becomes darker, so people look for refuge in the hedonistic pleasures and temptations of seedy Berlin. And the contrast between the grinding poverty induced by the hyper-inflation economy and the ability of the rich elite to indulge in escapist distractions all gets horribly exposed in the classic 'Money' song. According to *Cabaret*, love is something commended by the 'fat little pastor' whose advice goes out of the window as soon as hunger comes calling. It is money people need, not love or relationship. 'Money makes the world go around' – apparently.

So, what happens if money is in short supply? Where does security lie when the bank statement has turned red, the kids want expensive electronics for Christmas and all you want to do is get through to January without having fallen apart? How do you cope with the pressures that are put on children to 'have' what gives status and guarantees 'belonging' to the peer group? And how are you supposed to handle the (usually untested) assumption that everybody else is having a better time than you are and can clearly afford more expensive stuff for Christmas than you can?

The 'cash flow' crisis

We'll come back to Christmas in a moment, but it might be worth taking a slight detour into the world of debt. And how about this for a broad-brush, whistle-stop tour of the last 60-odd years? The generation that was born in the aftermath of the Second World War grew up in the optimistic atmosphere of a society rebuilding itself. When everything has fallen apart through war and the physical state of the country is poor, as the song says, 'the only way is up'. So the 1950s and 60s were all about recovery, construction and the building of a new and better future. The white heat of technological revolution was burning a trail and architects were playing with new materials for building roads and blocks of flats. But rationing didn't go out until July 1954 (nearly a decade after the end of the war) and people were growing the future while still experiencing shortages.

This fact is important. It reminds us that the energy for development was driven both by a commitment (a) to leave war behind and build for peace and (b) the daily experience of deprivation. The very rationing of meat made it clear that we can't have everything when we want it just because we want it. Families had limited money and had to budget. People had to learn to wait until they could afford it before they went out and got it. So, children were satisfied with what their parents could manage for them and adults generally saw this time as the laying of foundations for a better world/life for their children and grandchildren.

But, as affluence grew – and particularly as we moved into the acquisitive 1980s and 90s – the amount of money in most people's pockets grew. Perhaps more importantly, the debt culture began to grow and indebtedness came to be seen as normal or even noble – a statement of confidence about future affluence and trust in the economic laws on which our financial systems were built. 'Taking the waiting out of wanting' became not just an advertiser's slogan for a credit card, but the consumer reality for most people. You could buy anything now and worry about paying for it later. And Christmas brought together a pile of pressures: the blackmail that you are depriving your kids if you don't spend to satisfy their peer-driven demands; the easy and unquestioned availability of credit (which should always be called 'debt'); the whipping up of a commercially driven and artificial festival of consumer indulgence and obligatory cheerfulness.

It seems oddly ironic, then, that the central figure of Santa Claus himself is derived from St Nicholas (fourth-century Bishop of Myra) whose fame spread because of his alleviation of poverty . . . whereas today's Santa can have the opposite effect. Which brings us back to the first Christmas.

Maybe money *does* make the world go around

The first Christmas took place in a particular context. Bethlehem was a tiny place about four miles from Jerusalem and 70 miles as the crow flies from Nazareth in the north. Mary and Joseph didn't have a crow to fly on, so would have taken between three days and a week on foot or with the help of a donkey. Nazareth was in the northern hill country where the rebels hid out in between launching forays against the Roman occupying forces. For this country was a Roman colony and a tough assignment for whichever Roman got the job of managing it. The local Jewish leaders compromised with the Romans and the Roman forces knew they needed the cooperation of Jewish leaders. They also had a rather nasty line in executing rebels in the most publicly humiliating and cruelly tortuous ways they could devise – all based on what we have come to know as 'deterrence theory'. It didn't seem to work very well then either . . .

But for good Jewish businessmen like Joseph there was no escape from having to pay taxes to the occupying forces of the evil empire. This would, no doubt, have caused all sorts of religious and moral misgivings in the hearts and minds of the locals, but they still had to make decisions about how to keep their children fed, their businesses going and their homes protected. They wanted to be free and to be able to worship in freedom, being led by good religious and political leaders instead of the collaborators who saved their own skins by colluding with the enemy. So, Joseph and Mary did not go to Bethlehem from Nazareth for the good of their health; they went to register for the poll tax imposed by the Roman invaders whose very presence in the land put a question mark over the Jewish understanding of God, power and their own identity.

Mary was pregnant and the prospect of a 70-mile journey on foot could not have been an inviting one. Leaving Nazareth meant also leaving the business for several weeks (bringing loss of income as well as loss of productivity) and using already scarce resources for the unwelcome journey. They probably imposed themselves on their extended family for however long they needed to be there.

They then had to get their stuff together to get back home. Then take into account exile in hiding from the paranoid Herod and you begin to see the uncertainty and material challenge to this family.

In one sense, this is remarkable. If I was God, I would probably find a more secure way of guaranteeing my survival beyond babyhood in the fragile world we all know and love. But Jesus is born as a defenceless infant at a time of high infant mortality in a country being occupied and oppressed by brutal imperial forces and to parents whose marital relationship was questioned for the rest of his life and in circumstances that didn't exactly promise a thriving future. Mary and Joseph would also have had to face the economic and financial troubles and challenges every parent faces – in a society that had no social services and no unemployment or social security safety nets.

And all this goes to suggest that, indeed, money possibly does make the world go around – because we can't do without it and it constantly causes most of us a certain amount of grief – either because we haven't got enough of it or don't know what to do with it. But, the Gospel accounts of Jesus' birth indicate that God is no stranger to questions of profit and loss, work and play, vulnerability and exposure to what the world can throw at us. Shepherds risk unemployment by leaving their flocks and coming to find the baby; magi leave families and home to go on a star-led search for they know not what; Mary and Joseph count the cost of trekking to Bethlehem, but also have to count the potential cost of refusing to go. The first Christmas was fraught with uncertainty for many characters and was costly at lots of different levels.

I think this has something to say to our celebration of Christmas. First, it should remind us that God is no stranger to our own human experience. So, when we pray, we are not praying to a God who looks back at us dumbly or uncomprehendingly. Secondly, it

19

should encourage us that we can dare to refuse to play the commercial game at Christmas and, instead, invest in the relationships and common experience of celebration and sharing, thus recovering our own power from the advertisers and commercial drivers of our culture.

Some families will openly discuss how they are going to 'play' Christmas and will agree a spending limit on presents to be exchanged. Others will decide to invest in the time they spend together and to exchange tokens of love and appreciation. Some will struggle with the pressures from advertisers and children, but will learn that it is love that wins the affections of our children, not how much we spend on them. Yet others will go with the commercial and cultural flow and find themselves in January having created a short-term solution to one problem (affording Christmas) and a longer-term problem that is less easy to solve (lack of money and the fear that comes with indebtedness).

When I was at school I couldn't quite get my little head round the origins of Christmas. I knew that the tree was a pagan thing and that the date itself was a bit suspect, but I couldn't work out why Christians would simply take over other people's celebration and make it their own. Then I discovered that there is no harm in taking something that already exists and giving it new meaning and significance. Christmas comes just a few days after the shortest day (at least in the UK). It recognizes the darkness and miserableness of the winter and doesn't seek to minimize it. But it also has a bit of a laugh because the darkness isn't going to last: the days are going to grow longer and the spring is promised, even if there are cold and unfriendly spells to go through first.

In other words, Christmas was planted at the most significant and hopeful turning point of the calendar in the northern hemisphere. (I am sure this will have to be adapted for Africans and

Australians, but it certainly makes sense of the experience here in England.) Christmas trees point towards the heavens and beyond the current immediacy of our dilemmas. The darkness is challenged by lights that taunt it with the hope and promise of spring and new birth. And through it all there cries the challenge to defy the evidence of our eyes and live as if spring was coming. Christmas is about hope.

So, money matters. But it doesn't ultimately make the world go around. When the cash dries up we are thrown upon the love and generosity of those to whom we belong. It is our relationships that sustain us and keep us hanging on. Strip all the 'stuff' away and at Christmas we still can't help but celebrate the fact that God has come among us as one of us and shone a light into the darkness – a light that can be dimmed by circumstances, but can never be snuffed out.

4 GIVE PEACE A CHANCE

It is always hard to know just what actually happened during events that have since become almost mythical. On Christmas Eve 1914 the German soldiers in the trenches near Ypres in France started decorating their wasteland battlefield and singing carols. The truce that was called led to enemies exchanging gifts in No Man's Land and, if some stories are to be believed, a game of football. Christmas out of the way, they then resumed 'business as usual', killing each other in particularly pointless and brutal ways. The generals vowed that no such lull in the fighting would be allowed to happen again. They obviously decided that allowing the Christmas spirit to intrude into the area of human relations and politics would be detrimental to the important business of war and mutual slaughter.

What made the soldiers declare their own truce and play games? Was it simply that they were weary of all the mud and murder and needed a bit of respite – one that Christmas conveniently provided? Or was there something about Christmas itself and the haunting memories of hope for something better in the world than the usual horrors? Well, we don't know and we probably will never find out. But, for my part, I suspect it had something to do with what Christmas is and what Christmas promises.

John Lennon seemed to put this into words when he lay back in his honeymoon bed at the Amsterdam Hilton Hotel in March 1969 and explained to a reporter that 'All we are saying is give peace a chance'. He liked the phrase so much he wrote the song and it was released in July 1969 at the height of the anti-Vietnam War protests. Sometimes it is the simplest (maybe also the most simplistic) expressions that cut through the sophisticated rationales and arguments of powerful people and go to the heart of the matter. Long political debates about Vietnam and other political ventures – including the Civil Rights movement in the USA – produced acres of newsprint and filled the airwaves with discussion and polemic; but it was a simple invitation from the mouth of a rebellious Scouse musician that we still remember today: how about giving peace a chance, given that some of the other alternatives don't seem to be bringing us a lot of success?

We all long for peace, but we don't always think about what that peace might look like. Surely, we can't be so stupid or cynical as to think that peace really is simply the absence of war or conflict? Whether we are thinking at an international or local level or in terms of how we get on with our relatives, there is something in most of us that longs for an end to tension, the resolution of conflict and the freedom to live in peace and freedom. The problem is, however, that my idea of peace might not accord with that of my neighbour. Why not? Because in the real world peace involves agents who have competing or sometimes contradictory claims on time, space or place. One man's peace is another woman's conflict. So, it is not enough simply to think that if everyone was nicer to each other, peace would be the outcome. Peace requires hard negotiation, sacrifice, vision and shared values by those wanting to be at peace with each other. Peace rejects escapism.

Peace to his people on earth

One of the weirder features of the Christmas story involves shepherds, angels and a visit to the baby in the manger. There are two elements of this that we need to take a look at: the song the angels sang in the night and the identity of the baby in the manger.

As we have noted earlier, the shepherds were ordinary working men, out on the hills minding their own business – which was 'sheep'. What would you expect ordinary working men to do if the sky was ripped asunder and you were addressed first by an otherworldly being dressed in white and subsequently by a choir – no less – of singing angels? Given the political and economic situation in the land, songs proclaiming glory to God and announcing 'peace to his people on earth' might sound quite apposite. If everything is a bit of a mess and the future doesn't exactly shine with promise, the message you really want to hear is one of hope and resolution. But, would you really want to hear it from a bunch of angels who intruded uninvited into the routine of your night shift?

'Peace to his people on earth', although a welcome sentiment, might also have sounded a little bit optimistic. The Romans are there, occupying the territory, exploiting the land, taxing the people, dividing the citizens, oppressing the natives and generally doing what powerful imperialists do to annoy their subjects. Most resident Jews want them out, but some are doing quite well out of the arrangement. They are desperate for God to get glory – by booting the pagan Romans out and restoring the land (and the Temple and all that went with it) to the people who worshipped the one true God. They couldn't conceive of God being 'glorified' while the presence of the Romans made a mockery of the Jews' faith. So, when the shepherds heard the first part of the song they might have thought that, at long last, something was going to happen to sort things out once and for all.

The second part of the song might also have sounded hopeful, but the process might not have been so obvious. 'His people on earth' could only be at peace when they were free from their oppressors and able to demonstrate to the wider world that their God was the only god. So, if God's people were to have 'peace', presumably someone was going to have to start the rebellion that would see the Romans defeated and expelled from Israel. And, given past experience of such things, presumably also this rebellion would be costly and bloody. So, peace might be a lovely thing to hope for and be promised by an angel in song, but the ordinary working men on the hillsides would have wanted some clue as to who and when and where and how.

Fast-forward to the next bit and we find the shepherds wandering into town and visiting a baby. Now, just remember what we have previously noted: peace would require a costly struggle and the rebellion would need a leader. And here they are, looking at a little baby in a trough attended by rather bewildered and exhausted parents. It doesn't compute, does it?

Or, maybe it does.

Look differently

If we leap ahead in the story of Jesus, we find him in Mark's Gospel beginning his public ministry back in the hill country of the north and summarizing his message in four short phrases: 'The time is fulfilled. The kingdom of God has come near. Repent and believe in the good news.' In brief, what this is saying makes sense when heard in the context of what we have just observed earlier: Now is the time God is back among us. His presence is actually here among us now. But, to see it, you will have to change your way of thinking ('repentance' literally means 'change of mind') and spot the presence of God not in your liberation and in the resolution of your circumstances, but while they continue. If you can see the presence of God (in Jesus) even while your circumstances continue to be grim, then commit yourself – body, mind and spirit – to what you now see ... despite the evidence of the world around you.

In other words, can you only ever see God when your problems are solved, life is smooth and your prayers seem to have been answered? Or can you see God being with you even while your problems continue, life is a mess and your circumstances seem to tell a different story? Or: do the 'Romans' have to go before you can be convinced that God is with you?

And, I think this helps us to understand the shepherds and what was required of them. They would expect peace to follow a rebellion against the Romans; but they were led to an unprotected baby and not to a warrior. They were looking for God's glory to be evidenced by an act of power and might; but they were led to a place of apparent weakness and vulnerability. They would have to look differently at God, the world and themselves if they were to be able to spot the presence of God in a baby. They would have to take the massive risk of looking differently in order to see differently in order to think differently in order to live differently.

And Christmas present?

So, what might the experience of the shepherds have to say to us in a different culture and at a different time in history? Perhaps the first thing is to help us realize that God comes to ordinary people in ordinary places doing ordinary work and invites us to think differently about him and the world. So, there's hope for all of us. Perhaps the second thing is to recognize that we easily tame Christmas and become so familiar with the story that we fail to be surprised by it any more. If so, we have an opportunity to look afresh at it and ask new questions of it. And maybe the third thing is for us to question our own assumptions about what 'peace' means.

One of the subjects most explored in film and story regarding Christmas concerns the conflicts and tensions that can arise within families. Some of the stresses get accentuated at a time when families are thrown together and told they must be happy. So, the notion of 'peace on earth' is no longer just something vague about the resolution of international conflict, but comes closer to home – in fact, it comes right into the heart of the home. And it then asks us what it might mean for there to be peace on this particular piece of earth called 'our house'.

Of course, there are many people in our society and local communities who would love to have a family to be tense with. Loneliness – especially the sort that leads to a feeling of isolation despite living in a densely populated part of town – can be accentuated by the plethora of images of 'happy families'. Christmas is a time of year when the loss of someone close is felt most acutely and for many bereaved people the Christmas period becomes an endurance test in which grief and the powerful emotions of loss either get suppressed or drive them to a sort of withdrawal.

Peace in these circumstances involves a coming to terms with what has happened, the freedom to give expression to real emotion and being able to belong to a community that understands grief and its unpredictable power. But, I guess all of us bring to our Christmas celebrations a complex of needs and fears and lonelinesses – it is just that some of us either don't recognize them or don't want to face them.

As an aside, it is worth noting here the importance of a church community in offering a place for unconditional belonging – a community that is characterized by an absence of surprise when faced by messy lives and people riddled with contradictions. Every Anglican service begins with a common verbal admission that all of us are messed up and that we have no illusions about it. So, we are in good company and don't have to pretend to be more 'together' than we actually are. Confession is followed by hearing that God, who knows us and is not surprised, forgives us and sets us free to start again. This is liberating language for a community of people who no longer wish to hide or play the social games that push us into pretending to be what we are not.

Anyway, if there is nothing particularly romantic about our domestic tensions and pleasures, then this is the same for the family that is sometimes referred to as 'holy'. There are characters in this nativity story who don't all see things the same way, but they converge in all their bewilderment around a baby who they dare to believe might bring hope of a different way of being in this world. No instant fix to the world's ills, but the beginning of a process that would take time and be worked out through the natural run of time and space. This means that the dilemmas, tensions and celebrations of ordinary life have to be negotiated as they go along and the things that life throws at them be faced. Does that sound familiar?

I think this should be surprisingly reassuring to those of us who struggle with family life, the competing priorities we face and often fail to resolve properly, and the frustrations we sometimes feel when we can't sort everything out to our satisfaction or make everything better immediately. Peace, after all, has to be worked out in and through the little decisions we make together about all sorts of mundane and ordinary things. Recognizing that we may see things differently and that the process of changing our mind (the way we look and see and think and live) takes time and cannot be forced can help us when we feel our patience is evaporating in the heat of the 'Happy Christmas' cauldron.

Perhaps, even though the context is different, there can be the opportunity to create the space in which we declare a truce, sing some songs and have a game of something that takes our mind off the struggles and strife of ordinary life. We might not be able to lie in a hotel bed like John Lennon thinking up songs that will earn us millions, but we could give peace a chance – recognizing that the peace God offers does not take us out of the real world, but needs to be experienced within the circumstances of our lives and homes. Perhaps it starts with spotting the 'glory' of God and then experiencing the peace that comes from knowing that God knows.

5   O COME, ALL YE FRETFUL

Christmas is not Christmas without the ritual singing of certain carols. As we only get one shot at this each year, we have to get all the favourites in in one go. It's a bit like not eating curry for fifty weeks of the year and then having it for breakfast, lunch and dinner every day for a week. If you only have to go to one carol service, you probably won't know what I am talking about – but spare a thought for the clergy.

Most carols are OK. They try, within the constraints of several verses and an easily memorable tune, to capture something of the story of Christmas or the mind-boggling idea of God becoming human and living among us. And they do this with varying degrees of success for varying types and ages of people.

For example, I always find it a slightly bizarre sight when I see parents and grandparents at a nativity play singing 'Away in a manger' as if it actually related to reality. I can understand the little children being quite taken with the sort of baby of whom it can be said 'no crying he makes', but how can any adult sing this without embarrassment? I think there are two problems here: first, it is normal for babies to cry and there is probably something wrong if they don't; secondly, are we really to believe that a crying baby Jesus should be somehow theologically problematic? Or, to put it more bluntly, is crying supposed to be sinful?

Actually, I think there is an even more serious third problem. If we sing nonsense, is it any surprise that children grow into adults and throw out the tearless baby Jesus with Father Christmas and other fantasy figures? 'Once in royal David's city' has Jesus as 'our childhood's pattern' – even though we know almost nothing of his childhood apart from one incident when he was twelve years old and being disobedient to his parents – and invites children to be 'mild, obedient, good as he' – which means what exactly? This sounds suspiciously like Victorian behaviour control to me.

On the other hand, there are carols and poems that express in a single line what most of us struggle to put into a hundred or a thousand words. When the massive mystery of the incarnation is expressed in words such as the seventeenth-century poet Richard Crashaw's wonderfully poetic phrase, 'eternity shut in a span', the language invites deeper reflection, opening up the bigness of the Christmas event. They suggest that however hard we try to give verbal expression to the events of the first Christmas we can never do justice to their enormous profundity or significance. After all, how are we to put into mere words the eternal and infinite God who created the cosmos taking human form and living among us? It defies any and every attempt at comprehensive comprehension. If God can be reduced to a span, our minds can't reduce the whole business to the easily comprehensible.

Who let them in?

But, lets' get back to the story itself and the way the carols attempt to tell it – with, as we have seen, varying degrees of success. No carol service is complete without one carol in particular: 'O come, all ye faithful'. It has a great tune and the descant on the 'Sing, choirs of angels' verse sets the hairs on your neck tingling with excitement every time you sing it or hear it. It is a wonderful invitation to the faithful to come and worship. And that is where I have yet another problem.

When you look at the stories of Jesus' birth in the Gospels of Matthew and Luke, it is not the 'faithful' who come to see the baby and his parents. Shepherds are the great unwashed, those who cannot fulfil the regular religious rituals because they are always up on the hills, allowing the flock owners to do their religious stuff properly. Yet it is the shepherds who find themselves confronted by angels at their place of work and – surprisingly to them and to us – find themselves invited to be the first to see the baby.

Go a bit further and we find wise men (magi) – most probably astrologers from what we now call Iraq – embarking on a long journey from their home to discover this child as the one who would change the world. They were not good Jews. They were not Jews at all. They were pagans – men who were outside the covenant people of God.

In other words, it was not the 'faithful', but rather the 'faithless' who were given the privilege of visiting and identifying the child who would be seen as Emmanuel, God with us.

Now, read on in the Gospels and you find that all the people Jesus healed were ones whom the kosher people of God regarded as being unclean, unworthy or for some other reason outside the community of God's people. One of the things we are supposed to ask when we read the Gospels is: why are all the 'wrong' people responsive to Jesus and why do the 'right' people crucify him? It all seems upside down and inside out.

But this rams home the fact that when we come to the story of Jesus, we have to be willing to have our assumptions about God, the world and ourselves subverted. We have to learn to think differently about how things are and how they should be. And this means that we begin to see the 'wrong' people as the 'right' people and begin to understand on whose side Jesus came to be. Perhaps the carol ought to be re-written as 'O come, all ye faithless'.

But there is another possibility that includes both the faithful and the faithless. How about 'O come, all ye fretful'? Why? Well, look again at the Gospels and see how Jesus spent time with people on all sides of the 'faith' or godliness lines. He followed through the early promise of the shepherds and the magi by mixing with the rich and the poor, the powerful and the oppressed, the governors and the rebels, the young and the old, women and men, co-citizens and foreigners. And many of these people brought with them all the complexes of fear and anxiety, of illness and disability, of anger and resentment, of confusion and bewilderment at the lot they had been cast in life. A few examples might help us understand this.

A crippled woman

Luke tells the story of a woman who has been crippled for a couple of decades. She seems to be the object of local people's derision and neglect. After all, if she is so badly ill, she must deserve it – either because of her own or her parents' sin. So, apart from a lack of any social security system to support her, she also lacks the compassion of her neighbours. Imagine what that does to your self-respect?

While Jesus is teaching in a synagogue on Saturday this woman appears and Jesus spots *her*. Note that: Jesus spots her, not the other way round. He calls her over and heals her by word and touch. Now, you'd think everybody would be delighted for the poor woman and amazed at what has just taken place before their very eyes. Not a bit of it. The religious bigwigs get upset because Jesus has done it *on the wrong day*, the Sabbath, when no 'work' should be done. How is that for seriously missing the point? Instead of celebrating the healing activity of God, they give Jesus a hard time for having 'worked' on the Sabbath.

But the really significant element of this story comes later as Jesus sets about embarrassing what he calls 'the hypocrites' and refers to this woman as 'a daughter of Abraham'. In that one phrase, spoken in front of the very people whose religious duty it is to bring people to God, Jesus gives that woman a history, an identity, a future and a place of dignity in the community. Now, imagine what that does for your self-respect?

A young child

The adults are fed up. While they are trying to give their attention to the teaching and conversation of Jesus, the kids keep getting in the way and distracting them. Maybe they are playing around the legs of the audience and just irritating them the way only children can. The adults try to shoo them away so they can focus on the important stuff. But Jesus won't have this and calls one of the children to him. Setting the child in the midst of them, he then looks the adults in the eye and tells them that rather than shooing the children away, they would in fact have to become just like this child in order to fit in to the place where God's way of doing things rules.

It seems as if Jesus is trying to suggest that curiosity is at the heart of being a child of God. The tragedy of adulthood is that we have generally had the curiosity and inquisitiveness about the world beaten or bored out of us. But young children are always asking 'why?' and using their imagination to explore the enchanted world that holds so much mystery for them. Jesus seems to say that adults must lose some of their sophisticated cynicism and relearn the art of wonder and questioning and curiosity.

Zacchaeus

Tax collectors were collaborators in the pay of the occupying forces. Not a great place to start, if you want to gain the respect and love of the people. Zacchaeus was one of these compromised individuals who would have had no friends in the wider community and few in the community of tax collectors and collaborators: after all, who would trust someone they knew to be as untrustworthy as themselves? He made a good living from collecting for the Romans and adding large sums for himself.

Zacchaeus hears that Jesus is coming and tries to observe him from a safe distance – in his case, up a tree where he can peer over the crowd that would not make space for the treacherous toad they considered him to be. To his horror, Jesus stops at the tree, looks up and calls the traitor (by *name* – just how embarrassing is that?) to come down and prepare to offer hospitality. Zacchaeus could pretend to be hiding or deaf, but he does what Jesus asks and provides him with generous hospitality.

Now, this would have been annoying and embarrassing to the onlookers – especially the self-righteous onlookers. Why was Jesus choosing to spend time with and receive hospitality from such a nasty little man as Zacchaeus – a prime traitor to the cause – when there were other, more righteous people around? Why was he privileging such a toerag when he should be avoiding the contaminated people and mixing with the more holy ones? Did he not realize the danger of being infected, compromised or misunderstood by prolonged contact with such a disreputable man? Was he not worried about his own 'purity'?

We don't know what happened in the house of Zacchaeus. All we are told is that Zacchaeus went in as a despised bad man and came out later as a generous risk taker who had changed his ways and repaid those he had swindled. Instead of Jesus being contaminated by the bad stuff, the bad man was contaminated by the goodness of Jesus. Yet the 'righteous' people were indignant that Jesus had got his priorities wrong.

So what? Well, the reason the Gospel writers chose the stories of these particular people for inclusion in their narrative was precisely because they wanted the world to know that God is on the side of the bewildered and confused and fretful. If God is truly to be found in Jesus of Nazareth, then this God is not there for the self-satisfied, the religiously smug or the dogmatic nit-pickers, but for the marginalized, the weak, the problematic, the confused, the shamed and the social embarrassments. And that, I think, leaves enough room for most of us – perhaps especially when we approach Christmas with anxieties about family, money, food and self-respect.

This might sound a bit odd, but I think Christmas is most authentically celebrated by those of us who feel a bit of a mess and bring to the festival a bag-load of cares and complications. Christmas says, if only we can hear it, that God is on our side – not in some remote, airy-fairy religious sense, but by coming right down into the messy world we inhabit and saying in word and action, 'I am for you.' The Church is simply the community of people who fit this category and want to extend a welcome to anyone else who wishes to find company.

6 FAMILY FUN?

Families are great until they go wrong. But, for most people, an admission that families aren't always fun sounds like a confession of failure. We have to keep up the appearance that all is well in the particular nuclear family that is ours or our reputation might fall apart. I know families that are wonderful examples of good, healthy relationships based on respectful intimacy – and these are to be celebrated. But most of us also know of families that are not as healthy as they might be and we have friends or relations who could be thought of as casualties of family life. As David Copperfield remarks: 'Accidents will occur in the best-regulated families.'

I remember being asked many years ago to speak at a large gathering associated with a large church in the Midlands. The theme they gave me didn't warm my heart. They wanted me to do two sessions (a week apart) on 'A biblical understanding of the family'. I didn't get off to a great start when I declared confidently at the outset of session one that there is no such thing as a 'biblical' understanding of 'the family'. I remember getting through the first address and discussion, but I have no recollection whatsoever of the second – which possibly means it got 'unavoidably cancelled'.

The point I was trying to make is that there is no single pattern of family life in the Bible. We can't just read back into the text the assumptions or experiences we have in twenty-first-century Britain. In the Old Testament there is a variety of shapes to families, all of them patriarchal and involving lots of wives and no church weddings. Put simply, the assumption that 'family' equals one wife and a couple of children (one male and one female, obviously) owes a lot to the western model of the nuclear family; you won't find it in that form in the Bible (although it was moving that way in New Testament contexts). And why not? After all, the biblical books were written in cultures very different from our own. And, although we can distil principles of family life and marital relationships from the Bible, it is a bit arbitrary to suggest that we can locate a single model within its pages. (For example, most of us don't have 'households' such as those encountered in the Acts of the Apostles, which were extended family groups that included slaves and servants.)

This is more important than it might sound initially. I wonder if the assumptions we make about the 'normal' family are ultimately very helpful. Whereas it is indisputable that children thrive in a two-parent family in which the parents love and respect each other – and I would have no hesitation in promoting this as the best 'model' of family life – it is simply the case that fewer and fewer families live this way in the contemporary world. And that reality has to be taken seriously, not simply bemoaned by people who always wish the world was different from how it actually is.

One of the gifts brought by immigration in England is the experience of witnessing how extended families work. I know that Asian and African families are now being infected by the great freedoms of the cynical west and resorting to easy divorce and other 'lifestyle choices', but, as a student in Yorkshire in the 1970s, I was constantly amazed that I could get a meal or buy a loaf of bread at midnight from families who shared a home, a business, a car and the children – which is to say that all members of the family took responsibility for their part in all of these, including caring for and nurturing the children in the extended family. Belonging to a 'family' meant belonging to something bigger than the nuclear unit.

The contrast with my kids' generation in England could not be more stark. I remember asking my then teenage children and their friends if they had significant relationships with any adults other than their parents and teachers. The unanimous answer? 'No.' In fact, the only teenagers who did have such relationships with other adults were those who belonged to a church 'family'. It is true that the increased mobility of people in the UK in the last few decades has made it harder for extended families to live in close proximity. In my own case, our moving around the country has meant that we have never lived within close proximity to our parents or siblings. My wife's side of the family all live over 200 miles away from us; my own parents and a brother also live a similar distance away. I also have siblings on the south coast, in the Midlands and in Africa. I am not in direct or regular contact with any cousins or other relatives.

Now, let's not get carried away with romantic notions of perfect family life in eastern-modelled communities. But it is ridiculous to suggest that the increasingly common western models of family life are massively better. More children in the UK are now born out of marriage than to parents who are married. Divorce rates have shot up. The evidence clearly indicates that children thrive in stable families with two married parents. No amount of sneering at the inconvenience of such research will displace this fact. Accepting that this is not the shape of many families does not detract from the reality of the evidence – and does not suggest that only in such 'perfect' families can children thrive.

Family fantasies

But, why all this stuff about families when Christmas is all about bringing families together for festive fun? After all, you don't have to have your brain engaged to spot the thrust of all the

Christmas advertising aimed at creating (or appealing to) notions of family integrity and carefree happiness. The ultimate dream seems to be the nuclear family waking up on Christmas morning with a careless joy, kids laughing as they open their myriad of expensive and exquisitely wrapped presents at the foot of a huge (and expensive?) tree adorned with top of the range baubles in a large and beautifully decorated room of a (probably) large house. It all makes you feel warm and cuddly inside, even if it is a million miles from your own experience and bears all the marks of a romanticized fantasy.

The Beautiful South recorded a brilliant song called *One God* (from *Blue is the Colour*, 1996) in which they describe the feeling that the world is turning plastic:

> The world is turning Disney and there's nothing you
> can do . . .
>
> The world won't end in darkness, it'll end in family fun
>
> With Coca Cola clouds behind a Big Mac sun.*

This encapsulates most people's nightmare: rather than do some dramatic violence to our understandings of what it means to be a family, we'll just let it all go bit by bit while, anaesthetized by the drip of fantasy imagery, we find ourselves distanced from the dream. This is what led Don Cupitt, writer and theologian, to describe Christmas as 'the Disneyfication of Christianity' – an easy dismissal based on the stark difference between what we read in the Gospels and what we are presented with by our sentimental culture.

Some people can't wait for Christmas and the bringing together of scattered family members for a few days of celebration,

---

* Lyrics by David Rotheray and Paul Heaton, copyright © Island Music Ltd.

catching up and relaxing with all the social guards let down. For many this prospect is either unachievable or undesirable. For an increasing number of people in our own society, the prospect of 'family' celebration introduces a host of complications, problems and threats. How do you share out the kids over Christmas where multiple family units are involved – and the whole festival seems to ram home the fact that you've somehow messed it up? How do you look forward with joy to family friction, people who can't stand each other being forced into close proximity for a period? How do you cope with the expectations of 'having a great time' when you are worried about the expense involved, the demands of 'playing the family game' or pretending life is great when all you feel is fear about what lies ahead in the new year?

Well, you might accuse me of being miserable and trying to make everybody else join me in my pit of despair. But, you would be wrong. I love Christmas and love the family (parents, children and partners, friends) all coming together to celebrate and relax and play together. We do so as real people with real 'issues' and real relationships in the real world. The complexities are all there, as they are in any such gathering. And yet, I love and value the relatively short time we have together. However, years of pastoral work in ordinary parish communities have removed from my imagination any romantic ideas that Christmas is an unmitigated joy for everyone. You don't have to be a vicar for long to discover that some people dread Christmas because it accentuates their acute loneliness and makes it harder to accept that for days or weeks they will go untouched by any human hand. For others, Christmas promises exposure of their family rifts, their relationship failures or their material poverty.

A new family?

It is perhaps unsurprising, then, that a lot of churches now run Christmas dinners for elderly and single people in their community – not church community, but wider community. In my own episcopal area the churches also run a Floating Shelter for homeless people during the winter months and make something big of Christmas. I know many clergy – including those with young families of their own – who sacrifice their own exclusive Christmas Day and serve dinner to the lonely and isolated, thus demonstrating the ancient fact that Christians are called to love and serve the most vulnerable people in their communities. (The early Christians were admired and mocked in equal measure by the 'successful' Romans for caring for the widows and orphans who were not themselves Christians: Why do this and what can you possibly get out of it?) Crisis and other secular organizations also do fantastic work with homeless people at Christmas, but my concern here is with the churches.

In one sense this should not be surprising. Christmas, as we have already observed, is about God stepping out of what might today be called his 'comfort zone' and coming among us, stripped of rights and privileges. Christmas is about a real family, travelling a long way from home, coping with the anxieties of a stressful pregnancy and almost-failed engagement, having to consider how to feed each other and a baby, meeting strangers they had never met before and pondering an uncertain future. I guess they resigned themselves to simply getting through the next bit before being able to think about the substantial questions about what next and why.

So, families can have a brilliant time at Christmas and enjoy the company of those they love and love to spend time with. There can be lots of catching up and eating and drinking and laughing.

That's fine. But we must also somehow consider the fact that for many people this remains a dream and does not accord with the reality they experience each year. One consolation for them is that the God who gave birth to Christmas by coming among us in Jesus of Nazareth is no stranger to the stressful experiences we face.

Whatever our family circumstances, there are ways of making Christmas special and defying the fantasy makers. But they all mean having the courage to make space in busy diaries, face the incomprehension of others and be bold enough to carry them through. It is unrealistic to expect people who aren't familiar with the Christian lectionary (the readings that tell the story over a period of weeks through Advent and then the Christmas season) to radically change their routines for a period of weeks. But, for starters, it is possible to shape a Christmas in such a way as to recover not only its meaning, but also in such a way that it requires no money and only a bit of imagination.

Telling tales

We could start with simply making a time each day from Christmas Eve through to Boxing Day to read or tell part of the Christmas story to whomever is in the house. It could be done at breakfast or any meal where everyone is there together.

- Christmas Eve could cover the announcement to Mary and Joseph that their lives were about to change.
- Christmas Day could do the birth and the arrival of the shepherds.
- Boxing Day could tell the story of the magi.

Each reading could be followed by the singing or playing (a recording) of a popular carol. This would introduce a moment of reflection together to remember why Christmas is being celebrated in the first place. It won't take long, but is do-able.

One of the reasons for suggesting that the recovery of the 'story' is important is that these small rituals will in due time form the future memory of our children and, in turn, provide them with the tools for passing on a substantial Christmas to their children and grandchildren. We form the memories ahead of time by how we either do or do not do Christmas now. So, it is important, in the absence of any other ritual, to make a start somewhere – and to make a start that is achievable.

Remember the story of my experience in a South London primary school when the children had little or no idea of what the Christmas story was and couldn't distinguish between Jesus, Cinderella, Santa Claus and the elves? I cited this earlier simply to illustrate that many children have no idea what the story is. They get a bit of it in school, but many get nothing in their home and never get to a church. If our children don't learn the stories, not only will they be culturally disadvantaged (in relation to music, literature, art, history, geography, politics, philosophy, and so on), but they will also hit on a festival each December that is rootless and becomes an empty shell of a memory of which they were deprived.

7   HERE WE GO AGAIN!

It can't be much fun being an astrologer. The stars keep moving and you have to find ever new ways of saying the same generalized things time and time again to keep people suspecting there might be something in it. I have no idea what Iraqi astrologers were doing two thousand years ago or how they went about their trade. I probably should know more, but I just have to put up my hands and plead ignorance. We don't actually know a great deal about them generally, let alone the ones that set off to follow a particular star and ended up at the feet of a child called Jesus.

Of all the characters in the Christmas narratives, it is the magi to whom I relate most closely. I do not come from Iraq and I am not an astrologer: the only stars I gaze at are the musicians whose guitar playing leaves me stunned because what they do shouldn't be possible with only five fingers on one hand. No, I relate to the magi simply because they were men who followed their curiosity from one place to another, not knowing where they might end up or whom they might meet along the way, but still setting off on a journey filled with uncertainty and hope.

Of course, it isn't only astrologers who set off into the unknown. I was intrigued to read a journal written by a German television presenter called Hape Kerkeling who, following surgery in mid-life, decided to go on the pilgrimage to Santiago de Compostela in Spain. (The book is called *Ich bin dann mal weg: Meine Reise auf dem Jakobusweg*.) After an inauspicious start, he eventually got going and found the experience life changing. Not because it all went according to plan, but because he met people along the way and shared experiences to which he would never have been exposed had he not had the wit to start out on the journey in the first place. He set off into the unknown and frequently found himself leaning on the generosity and welcome of complete strangers who became friends along the way. It is a fascinating book because it tells the story of a journey that even in itself was transformative.

For an old English account of a journey you could do worse than read Chaucer's *Canterbury Tales* and see how that journey brought together a motley group of people who told stories to each other along the way.

Not so long ago another journey dominated the cultural consciousness of anyone with a television or a local cinema. The *Lord of the Rings* trilogy (although, to my mind, it seemed to go on for ever) told the story of a journey by some little people through all sorts of unwelcome territories in search of they knew not what. Millions of people who couldn't be bothered reading the thousands of pages of Tolkien's books (me included) watched the journey on the big screen as Frodo and his diminutive mates challenged the world and all its monsters in order eventually to get to Mordor. If my memory serves me well (and please don't make me watch them all again), they spent a good deal of the journey being frightened, bewildered, uncertain and wide-eyed with a sense of 'Oh no, something else is going to happen now, isn't it?'

But, the point is that they kept going. Even when they didn't want to be where they were, they overcame their fear and kept going. Even when they wished they could be anywhere but where they were, they still managed to stay on the journey. Tolkien wasn't just telling a great story that would work both on paper and on the screen; he was also facing his audience with the fact that life for all of us is a journey into an uncertain future. There are monsters ahead and encounters with people and experiences we would prefer not to have; but we either go through life wishing we were somewhere else or we get our heads down and look for the interesting or exciting stuff wherever we end up going.

Future shock?

I once heard an interesting take on this from a man who had left friends behind in the middle of a famine in Africa while he returned to a conference in England. He told his audience that when you are in a desert you should look for the flowers that grow only in the desert. If you spend your time in the dry place looking for flowers that grow only in fertile areas, you will be permanently disappointed. Look for the flowers that grow only in the desert and your experience becomes a unique and unrepeatable one.

Now, all this might begin to sound a bit twee or sentimental if we are not careful. But there is nothing romantic or sentimental about the lives most of us lead. When we get up in the morning we have no idea what might lie ahead of us in the course of the day. Even with a packed diary and an attempt to control life, you can never be sure what might happen. Most people who drop down dead never realize beforehand that this will be their final day on the planet. However, this uncertainty shouldn't sound like a threat, sending us running like frightened children for the security of mummy. This uncertainty can also hold out the possibility of exciting new experiences with wonderful new encounters with friends we would never have met had we not set out in the first place.

Coming back to the magi, I can't help but wonder what they were thinking when they set out on their pursuit of a particular star. But the lack of a certain destination did not stop them leaving home and seeing where they might end up.

It isn't clear at what point the magi found Jesus. Given that, on the evidence of the magi, the paranoid King Herod had all the boys younger than two years old slaughtered in an attempt to get rid of 'royal' competition, it is possible that, having escaped, the family were back in Nazareth and that Jesus was a little toddler when they eventually tracked him down. (Matthew's Gospel states that they found him only with his mother in their house.) I wonder if the boy they found was quite what they expected to find when they originally set out.

Travelling wise

The magi are good guides to the journey we take 2,000 years later in our own lives. As we recognized at the beginning of this book, the last couple of years have been really tough for many. People who had retired have had to think about working again, but at a time when unemployment is rising, the economy is contracting and businesses are struggling to keep going. For many younger people the future looks particularly uncertain because the jobs they hoped to take have disappeared, credit has been withdrawn and mortgages for first homes require big deposits – which, for a generation that has grown up on mandatory debt, easy credit and 'taking the waiting out of wanting' consumerism, has proved disillusioning.

In previous generations there was probably no such expectation of a relentless improvement in living standards or, indeed, any assumption of some 'right' to improved lifestyle possibilities. We have become accustomed to levels of remuneration and reward that have, in some cases, become disconnected from anything real. Hence, we find it hard to take when our expectations crumble to dust before our eyes. Yet our parents and grandparents should not be surprised by the current restoration of normality: they experienced one or two world wars, the threat of the Cold War and other interruptions to any notion of a consistent and inevitable road to affluence and security.

This has raised the question as to the object of our search for security. Nearly 1,500 years ago St Augustine observed that 'our hearts are restless until they find their rest in [God]'. More recently we have invested our security in more mundane and concrete objects such as the financial system, the banks, 'rights' and easy access to what we want to own. At least, this was true for those in our society privileged to have access to money; it wasn't true for the unprivileged underclass who could only see how the other half lived by buying glossy celebrity magazines and watching tacky television programmes. But the question remains and is a tough one: In what or whom do I put my faith for the future?

Getting real

Now, it might seem that we have strayed a long way from Christmas by wandering around the economy and noting the blindingly obvious fact that life has been (and, for many, continues to be) tough. But this actually brings us back right into the heart of what Christmas is about. Life is unpredictable and full of possibilities, some of them not very pleasant or convenient. It was into just such a world that Jesus was born: occupied territory where life was cheap; high infant mortality rates and low life expectancy; social and political turmoil and the potential for young men to get caught up in violence and rebellion; a life of hard graft as families would live from day to day, trying to get a meal together and provide for the basic needs of life. I could go on.

So, the Christmas story comes over as powerfully real. When the writer of John's Gospel says at the beginning of his account that 'the Word became flesh and lived for a while among us – we have seen his glory (presence)', he is saying something extremely challenging: this God has come among us in the real world that we all experience and we can never point the finger and tell him he has no idea what life is like for us. After all, this baby was going to grow into a young man whose father would die while he was a teenager (probably), leaving him to take responsibility for his mother, the family, their income and welfare. This is the boy who would become the man who (to the evident horror of his family who thought he had gone mad) went on a three-year excursion around his home country until eventually he met his end on a gallows. This is the child who opened people's eyes to the possibility that God is present among us when our circumstances are bad – not just when everything gets resolved.

And this, I think, is where it hits us 2,000 years later. We often look for God to sort out all our problems and deliver us from the consequences of living in a contingent world. But God does not kick the Romans out and make everything all right for us; rather, he comes among us where we are and walks alongside us, inviting us to see God, the world, our circumstances and ourselves differently. Rather than simply change our circumstances for our personal convenience, he offers to change us within our circumstances. And what does that look like?

With friends like these . . .

Well, Jesus called a group of people to dare to go with him on an uncertain journey that would eventually lead to betrayal in a garden, denial around a fire, death on a gallows planted in a rubbish tip, the horrible emptiness of a dead Saturday, the bewildering shock of a resurrection Sunday and the creation of a new community of people who would journey together into the future. Just as the magi travelled together in search of what would turn out to be a young child, so the disciples walked together and argued together along the way.

What is fascinating about this is that Jesus had no illusions about his friends. But he called them to walk together, despite the fact that they hadn't themselves chosen their travelling companions: Jesus did the choosing – their job was to make it work together and offer the watching world a vision of how a new community can be born in which the divisions of society are not replicated. It is in being part of (or connected to – however loosely) a local 'family' that we can find ourselves part of a wider community of people who support, encourage and walk with us through the hard times as well as the good times. And these people, because of their experience of the Jesus born in Bethlehem, pursued by magi and visited by shepherds, raised in Nazareth and killed in Jerusalem, see themselves as the hands and feet and mouth and ears of that same Jesus who called them to leave the security of home and set out on a scary journey.

Funnily enough, the 'Church' (as we now call it) is supposed to look something like this (although it doesn't always succeed) and there is at least one in every community in the land.

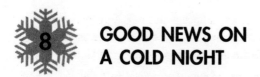

GOOD NEWS ON
A COLD NIGHT

I love the story of Santa's bad Christmas Eve:

> Everything is going wrong for him. He runs out of
> wrapping paper for the gifts and has to resort to bits
> of newspaper. Then he discovers there's no sellotape
> and has to squash the badly wrapped gifts into his
> sack. Tired and fed up, he throws his sack over his
> shoulder and limps out to his sleigh. Putting his foot
> on the running board, he hears a loud crack – his foot
> goes through, the sack falls off his shoulder and splits
> open as it hits the ground, throwing the now
> unwrapping presents out into the snow. 'It can't get
> any worse than this, can it?' he mumbles to himself.
>
> Looking up, he notices that the reindeer have gone.
> One is drunk, one is pregnant and two have done a
> runner. 'Oh no!' he complains, 'It can't get worse than
> this. I need a drink.' Heading back into the house, he
> goes to his whisky cupboard and finds it empty. At this
> point he hears giggling from the room next door, looks
> through and sees all the elves lying on their backs
> giggling – all stoned out of their minds on Santa's
> whisky. 'This is terrible', he says. 'What else could
> possibly go wrong now?'
>
> At this point Mrs Santa walks in and says to him: 'Oh,
> Santa, I forgot to tell you, my mother is coming for
> Christmas.' He looks up in despair only to hear her add:
> 'And she's staying for six weeks.' Just before he explodes
> in frustration and rage, there is a faint knock at the
> door. He opens it, looks down and sees a beautiful little

angel standing on the doorstep holding a Christmas tree. 'Hello!' she says brightly. 'Happy Christmas, Santa! Isn't it a wonderful day? Isn't it good to be alive?'

And that is the story of how the angel came to be stuffed on top of the Christmas tree.

Except that in some versions of the joke, it is a fairy that gets stuffed. How on earth do you get confused between an angel and a fairy? Well, it is obviously an easy mistake to make. Just as God is often confused with Father Christmas, the angels get confused with fairies probably because they apparently dress similarly and hover in mid-air while addressing human beings on the ground.

But, while we are at it . . . angels do seem to appear (usually on Christmas cards) in the most bizarre places. They are always white with curly hair, are dressed in white robes and have wings. Sometimes they appear to have trumpets or harps, but never a guitar. Even Robbie Williams once got carried away and got to number one in the charts with a song about them. But go into the pub and announce to the people in the bar that you've just had an encounter with one, and either the pub will empty or you'll be swiftly removed from the premises. For many people, angels are just like fairies or other imaginary friends and can, therefore, be consigned to the 'it's romantic for the children but has nothing to do with real life' drawer in the filing cabinet of life.

So, what are we supposed to do when we read or hear the Christmas story and can't avoid angels popping up from time to time, bringing various types of news to different people? Are we merely to tell ourselves that it's nice for the little children to have a bit of magic? Or should we just feel a little bit embarrassed – like we do when someone reminds us that we once wore flares and thought the Osmonds were fab? Should we cross our fingers and hope that the kids will grow out of it one day, just like we have?

Heavenly hosts singing earthly songs

Well, I think we are probably missing the point of angels by getting sidetracked into all sorts of speculation of what they either are or are not. Perhaps we ought to be a bit bolder than this and should ask ourselves what part these unusual creatures play in the stories of Christmas that we read in the Gospels. After all, these angelic beings are not simply wimps in white nighties, floating above the earth encouraging us to be nice to each other. No. They actually do embarrassing things. They appear before a soon-to-be-pregnant teenage girl and give her what most of us would regard as unwelcome – even bad – news. And just in case she is tempted to pretend nothing has happened, they even confront her fiancé and rub the bad news in. Later they interrupt the ordinary routine of a night's work for shepherds in the hills and invite them to come down into town to have their understanding of the world turned upside down in the presence of a baby.

Perhaps we are also supposed to notice in the text that instead of charming the cultured people of the day, God sends the best, most out-of-this-world choir not to the Friends of the Jerusalem Philharmonic Orchestra, but to these specimens of uncultured and unwashed humanity. The angels appeared to shepherds, not to the priests.

And that's the surprising place of angels in the Christmas story. They bring disturbing news to settled people. They roll back the curtain of the real world and open the eyes of working men to a vision of heaven. And they noisily and untidily bring good news to people who are willing to get off their backsides and come down the hill to a stable. The bad news of today's experience will soon and unexpectedly give birth to good news for the world. That's all. Angels just bring the news, open our eyes, have a party, and clear off again, leaving us to work out where we go from here.

Or, is it actually that simple?

The go-betweens

What the angels do is mediate between God and ordinary people who are being called to witness extraordinary things. My guess is that when the shepherds wandered in and saw the baby Jesus, they just saw . . . er . . . a baby called Jesus. I doubt that he had a halo round his head or that he spoke words of wisdom to his visitors. What the angels did was to change the way these ordinary people saw – and, therefore, enable them to look differently at the world and see new possibilities in it.

This, of course, is not new. Remember the Old Testament old-aged pensioner Abram who is invited to believe that, against all the evidence as well as the odds, he would father a nation. Instead of lying down and preparing to die, he set off on a long journey and made it possible for the promise to actually happen. He wasn't alone. Among other characters with sometimes surprising backgrounds was Moses the murderer: he was forced to confront his fears and take some responsibility for the liberation of his people from captivity in Egypt. After an unpromising start he led the whining people through a desert for forty years and kept alive the hope of a Promised Land when the others were becoming cynical. The prophets (such as Amos, Isaiah, Jeremiah) looked at what was going on around them and evoked in word and action (but, mostly, word) a vision of a different way of living together. They were ignored, so they just kept on adapting to the new circumstances and teasing the imagination of their people with a language of hope, a vision of a future that seemed unimaginable at the time.

In his public ministry Jesus began with a similar invitation. As we saw earlier, at the beginning of Mark's Gospel he goes to his home area and asks people to change the way they see and think in order to allow for the possibility that God might surprise them by his presence in the midst of their oppression. Up to this point they could only conceive of God being on their side (or even 'there') if he evicted the Romans from their land and gave them their place back; but Jesus challenged this notion that God is only there to make our lives feel better and solve all our problems.

So, when the angels get going in the Christmas stories, they are continuing a good tradition – or a habit of God, we might call it. They interrupt ordinary routines of ordinary people and invite us to look in a different direction, get off our backsides and move on in life. Usually this invitation is not welcome. The shepherds were 'frightened' by the heavenly choir singing to them before disappearing – isn't that what we call 'understatement'?

Spot the difference

But, as we saw in the last chapter, life rarely goes according to plan. We like to think there was a time in the past when everything was harmonious and life was ordered and comfortable – or that it should be like this at some point in the future once we have got over whatever the latest 'blip' is. This is fantasy. Normal life is unpredictable and gets interrupted when we least want it to. Bereavement is the most stark example of this. So, if this is normal, then what might we find ourselves hearing from the angels, the messengers of God's invitation to see differently?

We could start by looking at the world through the lens of the mass media. The media record what is abnormal in life, not what is expected. This means that, in the hackneyed example, 'dog bites man' is not news, whereas 'man bites dog' is. Almost by definition, the 'news' covered in the media is what is deemed 'wrong' or 'abnormal' in relation to our unspoken assumptions about what life should be like. The result is that we are confronted by news that is almost always bad and this becomes the 'wallpaper' of our minds when we think about the world. For example, statistics for some sorts of crime have not changed for a generation, yet many people feel less safe than they once did. We easily begin to think our way into a world of fear and caution and see the world as dangerous or bad.

The invitation of Jesus here would be to see through the lie that violence, fear and threat are normal – or that they have the final word. The baby born in Bethlehem grew into the man who defied the way of the world by contaminating it with love and mercy and generosity. When the 'wallpaper' betrayed a pattern of fear, Jesus said to frightened people, 'Do not be afraid: trust in me.' When it looked as if violent power ruled the world, Jesus said to bewildered people, 'They can take away your body, but nothing else; so, don't give them the power that isn't theirs anyway – lose your life for me and you will actually gain it.' And to people who thought they were condemned by both God and their society to second class (or even reject) status, Jesus restored them to health – and to taking responsibility in a culture that had previously made them a victim and shut them out.

This is still the case for us in a very different culture and at a very different time in history. The Jesus of the Gospels still invites (never forces) us to dare to see the world differently. We begin by seeing God differently – recognizing that he holds no illusions about us, but still loves us and gives himself for us – and daring to trust that he has made the world for more than suspicion, violence and fear. We join the community of people who, walking together a well-worn path but with a new vision of how life can be, are prepared to give their lives (like Jesus did) for the sake of other people. And we find that this company of fellow-travellers comprises such a weird variety of people from all sorts of backgrounds and with all sorts of dodgy stuff in their lives that we recognize in them and among them some of the people Jesus himself touched in the Gospels. In a world that for too long has promised success to the determined, the selfish and the greedy, we discover that there is freedom in living life differently – in fact, living it in the company of others who are also falteringly trying to follow the way and ways of Jesus.

So, the angels break into ordinary life and invite us to make a change in our life. No one could force the shepherds to walk down the hillside and into town. That was their choice. The angels had done their job and disappeared back to wherever they had come from.

9 THE LOBSTER IN THE STABLE

People of my generation who grew up on the innovative comedy of Monty Python's Flying Circus will remember the very funny sketch in which Michelangelo has to justify his version of 'The Last Supper' to the Pope. Apart from the 28 disciples and other inventions, Michelangelo uses what he calls his 'artistic licence' to introduce a kangaroo to the painting. The sketch has the Pope ordering the reluctant artist to go back to the characters actually mentioned in the Gospel accounts of the event. You can see it still on YouTube and it makes me laugh every time I see it.

I was reminded of this when I saw the Richard Curtis film *Love Actually*. Love it or loathe it, there is a wonderful scene when Hugh Grant (as the Blairite Prime Minister) goes to a school Christmas nativity play and finds himself sharing the car with Martine McCutcheon and a four-foot lobster. The lobster has a part in the play. That's right: the nativity play has a lobster in it.

I have been to many nativity plays in my time – it goes with the territory. And I have to confess to having witnessed some bizarre extrapolations from and interpretations of the story told in the Gospels of Matthew and Luke. Whereas there are only ever three magi, or wise men (although Matthew doesn't tell us how many there really were), there are often a dozen shepherds, hundreds of angels and, to make sure no one gets left out, a whole flock of young children dressed up as sheep. They don't do a lot, the sheep; they just sit on the stage and look bored. But at least they get a part.

But I have also seen a child pretending to be a snake, a teacher being a tree, two kids fighting over which end of the cow was preferable and, most intriguingly, a grizzly bear. Now, where do these come from and what is it that allows a teacher to come up with such characters for a play that is supposed to tell the story of the birth of the Saviour of the world? Or is that, in fact, the problem? Has this story become so detached from reality that it has become even less than a fairy story (remembering, of course, that you can't change a single detail of a fairy story without inciting rebellion among any audience under five years of age)? Is it thought to be so unreal that characters can be introduced or invented at will or in order to keep happy otherwise offended young thespians?

Making it real

I have never actually seen a lobster in the stable. I did once see a real young mother and baby and it stunned the children and adults into silence. It was in the parish where I was the vicar for eight years and we had so many people coming to carol services and other Christmas events that we decided to do a Christmas Eve afternoon 'service' for the children and young families. The ancient church was incredibly moody anyway, but at Christmas it lent itself to a sense of mystery. The building had stood there for over 1,000 years and the walls themselves seemed to have absorbed something of the worship and prayer and experience of people whose lives had been lived out in and around that place. So, each December we tried to present the Christmas story afresh – rehearsing the familiar while trying to shine a new light on the events and significance of that first Christmas.

One year the team of people conceiving and organizing the service decided that they wanted a different sort of 'tableau'. The chancel (front section of the building) was divided from the nave (main part of the church) by a medieval rood screen and this was covered in decorated fabrics, thus providing a visual backdrop to the telling and acting of the story before the congregation. Shepherds were there – and angels and bystanders. The drama unfolded, acted out not by the children, but, this year at least, by adults. Then we came to the end of the story and the search for the baby. The children and their parents were invited to leave their seats and journey like the shepherds and magi to see what had happened in Bethlehem. They slipped through the 'curtain' covering the rood screen and stood open-mouthed in silence as they saw what lay before them.

One of the first young couples I had married in the parish had by now had their second daughter. They had agreed to bring their two children and dress up as Mary and Joseph and place their baby in a wooden crib in the semi-darkness of the chancel. When the children and adults went through the screen they were confronted by a real young family and a very real baby. (OK, it was a girl. But she was wrapped in swaddling bands and nobody could tell the difference.) The effect was stunning. It reduced everybody to silence and many people said they felt they had wanted to say or do something to the young 'holy family', but didn't know what or how or when.

None of this was expected and I was taken aback by the emotional response of those who returned to the main body of the church 'by a different route'. I still don't fully understand it; but I think it had something to do with the apparent 'reality' of the nativity scene. Instead of being faced with more kiddy stuff that replicates the old familiarities (a doll in a cardboard box, for example), we were faced with a real baby and real adults in a real space. Whatever the reason, it had a profound impact and brought the whole story refreshingly and challengingly alive for many people who thought there was nothing new to be known about Christmas.

In one sense, none of this should be surprising. Christmas is basically about God not sitting a million miles above all the muck and bullets of the world we know, suitably protected from the messiness or uncertainties of the world the rest of us live in, but coming among us as one of us. So, being confronted by real flesh and blood human beings instead of a doll brings it home that the original family in the stable must have had faces and voices and all the other things that make us unique.

In another sense, I think the reaction of people to the 'real' family behind the screen was possibly attributable to a realization that Jesus cannot be reduced to the level of Father Christmas and the elves. As we noted earlier, God goes straight out of the window at the same time as Santa Claus when many people are teenagers (or earlier). God gets lumped into the same category as the fairy on the Christmas tree and doesn't have to be taken seriously any more. The problem with this, of course, is that often what gets rejected as children does not get re-examined or recovered as adults. Adults face a complicated world as adults, but their understanding of Christian faith doesn't grow up with them into adulthood.

What many adults reject about (their fantasy of) Christianity would also be rejected by most Christians. My argument here is that adults who rejected the 'fairy story' notion of God and Christmas when they were younger need to be invited or enabled to re-examine Christian faith and the credibility of the Christian story afresh as adults – bringing appropriate adult intellectual, experiential and emotional questions to it all. Otherwise we leave many adults rejecting a childish faith that most of us would not recognize as adult, credible Christianity anyway.

And this is where the nativity plays come in. There is a danger in simply repeating the old story (as we have imbibed it), but trying to update or renew it by introducing all sorts of weird innovations. What you end up with is a story that bears little or no relation to the narrative in the Gospels and a portrayal of Christian faith that looks decidedly odd. The lobster might be a fun addition to the nativity tableau, but it certainly demonstrates that the plot has well and truly been lost somewhere along the way.

The other thing that surprised me about the response to our 'real' nativity in the old parish church was that people spoke about wanting to 'worship'. They clearly didn't mean that they wanted to bow down at the feet of the young family behind the screen and offer them ultimate adoration. But the seeming reality – and the window it opened on their own spirituality – prompted them to want more, to go further. One couple told me that they didn't want to leave the chancel or go home, but wanted to stay there and 'go deeper'. I don't think there was anything spooky or odd about this reaction; I think they just began to experience what worship is all about.

A worthy response

Let's put it slightly differently. What do you imagine the shepherds did when they got into the stable (or lower room of the house, as it probably was)? We understand that they 'worshipped', but what did that look like? What did they actually do? Did they open a liturgical book and sing a hymn? Did they kneel down and pray – and, if so, what did they say? Or did they prostrate themselves before the baby and mumble things under their beards? I have absolutely no idea because we are not told what they did or how they did it.

But it does bring home the point that an encounter with the mystery of God coming among us – however this is pressed home to our tired and cynical minds – awakens something in us that demands more. Or maybe it makes us want to search more. I think this is the yearning expressed in those words of St Augustine already mentioned, 'Our hearts are restless until they find their rest in you.' Catching a glimpse of the powerful mysteriousness of the creator and sustainer of the cosmos contained somehow in a real baby in a real manger in a real house in a real town in a real country in the real world clearly does make many people want to stop and ponder the bigness of it all.

And this is what many of us would call 'worship'. Worship isn't primarily things you do in a service in a church. It is possible to sing and read and pray and never to have an experience of worship itself. For worship, while rooted firmly in our experience of this world, takes you beyond your present world and opens you up to the dimension of God's bigness and awesome humility. Here, after all, we have the creator, described by Richard Crashaw as 'Eternity shut in a span' – God come among us and vulnerable to all that the world can throw at him or the rest of us. It is just very hard to get your head round – and staying with that sense of awesome mystery is where true worship begins.

I think this experience is more common than we often realize. The Church doesn't always do people a service by reducing worship to participation in a service. The job of the Church is to create the space and the places where people can find themselves exposed to this enormous mystery that is the God who comes among us as one of us. It is to open our minds to wonder – to tickle the imagination so that we become dissatisfied with the banality of the common nativity performance by little children whose job seems to be to give their parents and grandparents a warm feeling that everything is OK. Worship begins where we know there is more and deeper and broader; but we have just glimpsed it and its beauty haunts our imagination, inviting us to move beyond the superficial and tangible 'stuff' of a predictable Christmas.

Mind your faith

I believe very firmly in the need for an intelligent and intellectual appropriation of Christian faith. Christianity is not – as one six-year-old child described 'faith' – believing things that aren't true. Rather, Christian faith deals with the real world and God's engagement with it in real time and real space with (and through) real people with real bodies and minds and voices. In other words, Christianity must be credible in the market place of ideas, but it can never simply stop there. The nativity experience demonstrates that we only get so far with our knowledge and understanding of the story; we can easily find ourselves compelled or teased to go deeper in pursuit of the God who came among us in Jesus of Nazareth. And that leads us into the contemplation and celebration that we call worship.

Stuff the lobster. Bring back the reality. Perhaps we need to recover the nativity play as something to be done by adults for children and not the other way round.

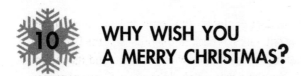

10 WHY WISH YOU A MERRY CHRISTMAS?

I was delighted to read in the newspapers that Ariane Sherine, *Guardian* columnist and the atheist who created the campaign for putting agnostic adverts on Britain's buses, was editing a book to celebrate an atheist Christmas. Why delighted? Well, mainly because she has got together 42 famous atheists and it seems that most of them are comedians. So, it should be very funny as well as exposing more of the atheist mind to public scrutiny. Let's face it, if we are going to do this sort of philosophy, we might as well have a laugh while we are doing it.

There is a rumour out there that Christmas would be great fun if Christians didn't keep spoiling it by bringing God into it and making it all serious or depressing. Like most rumours about anything in this world, it is always possible to find some people who will confirm the prejudice and illustrate the truth of the rumour. It would be stupid to pretend that there aren't any sad Christians who are never happier than when they are miserable. It is as if they heard Jesus say that he had come in order to wipe the smile off our faces and turn us back to concentrating on being miserable sinners. But, like most rumours, it would be stupid to extrapolate from the anecdotal few to the majority who don't fit the prejudice. (And the same goes for atheists, of course.)

But I think this is what lies behind some people's desire to recover the paganism that Christianity usurped a couple of thousand years ago. Every Christmas journalists hungry for the quirky stories dig up people who wish to dump the Christian accretions and get us back to celebrating an unadulterated yuletide festival with its evergreen trees, cycles of life stuff and the turning at the solstice from the dark winter to the fertile light of the coming spring. This, it is felt, takes us back to the origins of the December winter celebrations, reconnects us with the earth and its natural seasons and rhythms and gets rid of all the superstitious nonsense that Christianity imports to it. As a heart cry for simplicity and a rejection of all the commercially driven consumerfest that Christmas has become, it is not hard to have sympathy with its protagonists. After all, Christmas can easily be seen to bear little relation to any celebration of anything other than schmaltz and money and things and alcohol.

The charge brought against a Christian Christmas by neo-pagans is that all the religious stuff is unnecessary and that, anyway, Christmas was stolen by those ruthless Christians in the first place. Well, there is a certain truth in that charge. Christians were extremely adept at starting where the local culture actually was and shining a new light onto its already-existing practices and social customs.

A good example of this can be seen in the New Testament book of Acts which tells the fast-moving story of Paul (the energetic and visionary early church leader – and writer of half the New Testament). Acts 17 tells how he went to Athens and got into lively debates with pagan philosophers. It is striking that he starts not with God and the Bible, but with the Greeks' own poets and mindset. Like Paul, early Christians took the human celebration of life's mysteries (life and death, fertility and sterility, summer and winter) and filled them with colour. It was as if they were saying: 'You search for hope and meaning in the sterility of your experience? Well, the God who raised Jesus from death can be trusted to look after you in life and death, too.'

So, the Christmas tree wasn't thrown out as a pagan symbol that would corrupt the pure Christians if retained. It was re-signified –

that is, given a new meaning. 'Look through the evergreen tree and see in Jesus Christ the possibility that the God who has come among us remains "fertile" through all the seasons and rhythms and seeming caprices of our ordinary lives.'

So, you can celebrate Christmas as the turning point of the year, if you wish; you could go even further, though, and encounter the faithfulness of the God whose consistency through life and death can be trusted – whatever the circumstances of your life at any point in time. In fact, you can go even beyond that encounter and find yourself loved by the God who came among us in Jesus and showed a new way of being to those with eyes open to see. When Richard Dawkins claims to love Christmas as a 'cultural' festival (with absolutely no integrity or content, obviously), perhaps he is simply unable to shake off the 'myth' that life must hold more and cannot simply be accounted for in purely material terms.

Yet, this is where I and many other Christians would want to stand up and shout that Christianity is at the very least a 'materialist' faith. Christmas, at its very roots, screams that God is not immaterial – a sort of remote and wispy 'essence' – but takes matter and time and space so seriously that he enters into all its limitations and makes himself vulnerable to all that being mortal in a contingent world means. We can never shunt God off into some other 'spiritual' world which claims to be more 'real' than what we have on earth: that owes a lot to Plato, but nothing to Judeo-Christian assumptions about life and the world. Indeed, we would want to go even further and claim that it is only through Jesus of Nazareth that we really catch a comprehensible glimpse of 'what God looks like'. (I once summarized both Christianity and the Bible in these terms: If you want to know what God looks like, look at Jesus. How do we know what Jesus looks like? Read the Gospels and look at the people who claim to be his Body. In other words, Christians should reveal something of what people in the

Gospels experienced when they touched, listened to or argued with Jesus.)

Christmas, then, is an unashamed celebration of what is down to earth and fully grounded in the experience of the world as we know it. So, I have no problem in encouraging everyone to party. Not only is winter turning to spring (eventually) and light dispelling the darkness, but God has shown his face among us and invited us to join his celebration of new life and new hope right here in time and space and place.

Now, this might seem like a bit of a digression, but two further things might well be said here in order to clarify and dispel a couple of misconceptions that can be found within the Christian community as well as outside it.

First, Christianity is not primarily about what *we* do; rather, it is about God taking the initiative and coming to us. Right from the Garden of Eden onwards it is always God who comes looking for us – not the other way round (surprisingly). In Jesus, God comes to us and in the imagery of the Book of Revelation the 'holy city' comes down from heaven to earth – not the other way round. So, Christmas represents the most vivid and physical working out of God's nature: coming to us and being one of us, among us.

Secondly, partying is not a sin. One of the criticisms of Jesus by his own religious contemporaries was that he ate and drank and partied with all the 'wrong' people. He even got a reputation for being 'a glutton and a drunkard' – probably envious scorn at his ability to enjoy himself with people who knew how to enjoy themselves. But this shouldn't come as a surprise to anyone who has read the Gospels because Jesus' public ministry involved the announcement to those around him that God's presence was among them and the appropriate response was to celebrate. In fact, Jesus complained about people who missed the point of their faith and got obsessed with nit-picking; those who forgot their story and the original point of (for example) the Sabbath rest; those who were still behaving as if they were waiting for the 'bridegroom' to come when the wedding was already in full flow and they hadn't even noticed.

So, that is why Christians will want to encourage a great celebration and will reject any notion of killjoy miserable dampening of laughter and joy. But this has to be real and not just some form of escapism from the problems of the previous year or the realities of a hostile world.

Why, then, wish you a merry Christmas? Because this is when – despite all the consumerism and distractions – we want everyone to catch a glimpse of God's recklessness in coming among us in Jesus and thereby affirming the world and its people. What is important in all this, however, is that we should be dissatisfied with the guff that goes with the festival and recover our sense of wonder and gratitude and mystery and worship. Not primarily because it will make God feel better about what he did, but because it makes us more fully human and more authentically in tune with the world and the one who loved it into being in the first place. Christmas, we might say, is for life – and not just for Christmas. And it is life-giving, not laughter-draining.

Hang on a minute!

Now, some people are going to stop at this point and ask a very good question: 'How can we trust all this?' After all, many people express a great deal of scepticism about the veracity or accuracy of the Gospel accounts that bring us the Christmas story in the first place. How can we trust documents written by people who were already persuaded of the identity of this Jesus anyway? How can we handle documents that contain such odd elements and characters? Shouldn't we just accept that it is a nice story and not take it any more seriously than that? And, as the children enjoy it, it doesn't really do anyone any harm, does it? So, let's just have a good time, tell a few fairy stories (or 'myths') and leave out the embarrassing bits – the bits about Jesus, shepherds, angels and wise men.

Well, I think it is fair to say that this is naïve and is evidence of ignorance. It is amazing how many critics offer their opinion without having read the texts themselves. Responding to the charge that the 'history' of the Gospel accounts cannot be trusted because of the prior commitment of the writers, Tom Wright (now Bishop of Durham and a leading historian and theologian) writes: 'Of course the gospels are written from a point of view; so is all history. Christian faith is no more necessarily misleading as a point of view than modern agnosticism or atheism. Would you trust a book on Beethoven written by someone who was tone-deaf?'*

The story that lies at the heart of the Christmas story is one that powerfully affirms human life in the real material world, showing God becoming part of it and subject to it. The baby born in the stable is there to be recognized, but the fact that God looks as weak and vulnerable as this should also shock us and make us think again about who he is and how he is. And this leads us to the recognition that a genuine celebration of Christmas will also challenge us to allow the baby to grow up into the man he became. Jesus did not get crucified because he told people to be nice to each other; they nailed him because the vision of God and the humanity and the world that he embodied and represented was simply too threatening. If anything, the Christmas narrative

---

* N. T. Wright, *Who Was Jesus?*, SPCK, 1992, p. 95.

in the Gospels tells us that the challenge (and encouragement) of Jesus was visible right from the beginning.

I guess this means that Christmas becomes the beginning of a journey that takes us with Jesus and his friends through the Gospels to the cross and Easter and beyond. But we have to start somewhere. Christmas, celebrated well and with great joy and excitement, can be that first step.

AFTERTHOUGHT

This might seem an odd thing to do at the end of a book, but we have considered Christmas from different perspectives, yet missed a crucial bit out. It is worth coming to it at the end because it shines a light on all that follows in the Gospel narrative and all we have considered in this book so far.

When Mary is confronted by an angel and told she is to become pregnant with a baby who will become a world changer, she doesn't respond in a way I might have expected. I would have screamed. Or, maybe, laughed at the ridiculousness of it. Mary clearly had little option but to 'ponder these things in her heart': what else would she have done with the information – especially before her bump began to show?

Mirroring the song of Hannah the mother of Samuel in the Old Testament, Mary apparently burst into song. A song of joy? A song of hormonal emotion, perhaps? Or a song of gratitude or lament? No, none of these. She sings what has become known as the Magnificat. The problem with the Magnificat is that it has been set to music in some utterly wonderful and beautiful ways. But the beauty obscures the powerful and world-shattering content of the words. The full text can be found in Luke's first chapter, but here is a short extract:

> My soul magnifies the Lord,
>
> and my spirit rejoices in God my Saviour . . .
>
> He has brought down the powerful from their thones,
>
> and lifted up the lowly;
>
> he has filled the hungry with good things,
>
> and sent the rich away empty.

According to Mary's song, this child will grow into the man through whom God will transform the world. The powers will be challenged and a new way of looking at the world will be offered. In this song the powerful will be brought down and the lowly will be raised up. The 'rich' will be sent away empty-handed while the poor will find themselves satisfied at last. Those who are self-satisfied and proud will find their smugness evaporates in a moment.

Not exactly a nursery rhyme, is it? This is deeply subversive of the way of the world that thinks that might is right, that money always speaks or that power is a possession. And it is significant that this song picks up on the whole Old Testament tradition before setting the theme for the ministry of the child she is to bring into this world. Jesus will not die for telling people to be more thoughtful to animals and children; they will crucify him because he will challenge not only the people who run the world, but also the assumption that this is the only way the world can be. He will show how it is possible to think differently about the world and live differently in it, not being put down by its injustices and cruelties, but living according to a different rule and, therefore, being free.

In his first sermon (according to Luke chapter 4) Jesus picked up on this challenge and applied the words of Isaiah to himself: 'I will bring good news to poor people. I will proclaim to captives that they can be free. I will enable people who have been blind (to love?) to see clearly for the first time. Oppression can be challenged – and not necessarily with violence. I will show the world that this is God's way – you don't have to play the game that says the powerful always have power over you.'

Christmas, then, is not tame. If it is celebrated properly, it will be seen as a challenge to the dodginesses of the world we know. It will remind us of what it is to be truly human (as Jesus saw it) and consequently reorientate us for the coming year – setting our feet on the course that gives us the courage not to have to play the commercial games or perpetuate the value systems that underlie our culture. That is why being free from this stuff while living in it should be the cause of joy and a great deal of serious partying. The old ways have been challenged and ultimately defeated – so get out there and celebrate the birth of a new way of living.

In his live concert in London on 17 July 2008 the great Leonard Cohen spoke of his own journey through a variety of drugs (some medicinal). Then he said this: 'I've also studied deeply in the philosophies and religions, but cheerfulness kept breaking through . . . There ain't no cure for love.' This is both funny and tragic. It assumes that the search for authentic spirituality is inevitably miserable and unrealistic, or even anti-human.

Cohen spent a decade in a Buddhist monastery up a mountain and wrote some wonderful poetry there. But maybe the search for individual self-realization is futile when pursued for its own sake and somehow in isolation from the real world. Christmas says something different: you find yourself and your true humanity when you see through the eyes of the baby born to die at Calvary; and this takes you on a journey, not alone, but with a load of other people whom you have not chosen. In this uncomfortable and self-denying pilgrimage you will increasingly find the courage to live differently in this world and not to be intimidated when people think you are naïve or stupid.

One day the banks were considered to be the most reliable institutions in the world and bankers topped the polls of the most trustworthy people in society. Almost overnight that edifice of confidence collapsed and bankers (along with their industry) became almost vilified. Is this an example of how the mighty encourage us to live with an illusion of sufficiency, but how the world can change very quickly? The world need not be as we have been led to believe it inevitably has to be.

That is what we are celebrating at Christmas with the birth of the baby. The commercial driver of the festival actually neutralizes this vital challenge to money and power. There is no better reason than this for joining with other people who glimpse that God has something better for us in and beyond the present reality and calls us to celebrate it.

Merry Christmas!

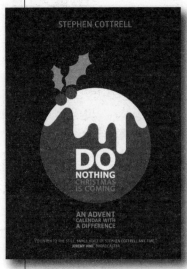

POCKET PRAYERS
FOR ADVENT & CHRISTMAS

Compiled by Jan McFarlane

With the run-up to Christmas among the busiest times of the year, it's not always easy to keep in mind the mystery and meaning at its heart. *Pocket Prayers for Advent & Christmas* is designed to help you make a space in the day to explore the rich tradition of festive prayers, carols and poems that millions still flock to church to hear.

Providing a prayer for each day of Advent and Christmas, this new addition the popular *Pocket Prayers* series offers a fresh selection of material that will comfort and challenge, helping you consider afresh the message of Christmas.

ISBN 978 0 7151 4196 0

Jan McFarlane is the Archdeacon of Norwich and the Diocesan Director of Communications. She is a regular presenter and contributor on local radio and has presented for ITV's *Sunday Morning* television programme.

What Am I Doing Here?
A BEGINNER'S GUIDE TO CHURCH

Hilary Brand
with illustrations by Dave Walker

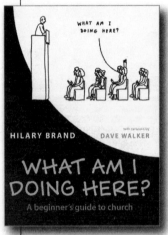

ISBN 978 0 7151 4161 8

Have you ever wondered what church is all about? Ever found yourself in a service wondering what on earth is going on?

Whether you're completely new to church or have been coming to church for a while, this little book is here to help you!

With a down-to-earth style and subtle humour, *What Am I Doing Here?* takes you through an Anglican Holy Communion service, demystifying what happens – and why.

'Realistic and funny and debunks some of the myths about church'

Nick Baines

'Most books nowadays explain why people don't go to church any more. It is good to find one that explains why people still do.'

Ian Hislop

Hilary Brand is author of *The Sceptic's Guide to the Bible* and the best-selling Lent course *Christ and the Chocolaterie.*

Dave Walker is the UK's best-known Christian cartoonist. He draws a weekly cartoon for the *Church Times* and is the author of *The Dave Walker Guide to the Church.*